Writer's Prompt Journal

This creative writing exercise belongs to:

____

How to use this book:

This book contains a variety of prompts meant to trigger a two page creative writing exercise.

The intention is not to create amazing art, but to break the ice and start getting words on the page.

Title your piece once it is complete.

Where a prompt 'includes' an item, this can be part of the plot, setting or just a part of the discussion, as long as that element finds its way into the final piece somewhere.

Title: ______________________

Prompt: Your characters are on a long journey and each stop has had its own trials. Describe the fourth stop on their journey. Include a spork.

Title: ____________________

Prompt: Retell a myth or fairy tale only this time change the ending. Really explore a character's motivations.

Title: ______________________________

Prompt: Write a story about a piece of kitchenware being used for something other than its intended purpose.

Title: ______________________

Prompt: Write about a character whose actions are completely at odds with their interior thoughts. Show the disconnect between the two.

Title: ____________________

Prompt: Write about an unbelievable event or coincidence. (Try and use an example from your own life as the basis for this story.) Include Finland.

Title: ______________________________

Prompt: Write about two former lovers who are forced to interact. Positive or negative, what outcome of this conversation feels right? Include a river.

Title: ____________________

Prompt: Setting – describe a place from your youth to a character who has never seen it before.

Title: ______________________________

Prompt: Write a letter to yourself from the perspective of a character who strongly opposes an opinion you hold. Why do they think you are wrong?

Title: ______________________

Prompt: Write about a dream moment in the spotlight (winning an award, acting in a TV show etc.). Describe it in great detail for the protagonist.

Title: ______________________________

Prompt: Biography – on the two pages provided, capture a complete character's life story. This can be as wild or as mundane as you like.

Title:

Prompt: Build a picture of a character then let them do whatever they like – give them free reign to express themselves. Include a food item.

Title: ______________________________

Prompt: Write a piece that captures the atmosphere of preparing for a birthday party as the background to your story.

Title: ______________________________

Prompt: One hour challenge – write about dramatic events that unfold and resolve in the space of just one hour. Include a hat.

Title: ____________________

Prompt: Write a story in four parts, one for each season. Let your piece capture a plot that unfolds over a whole year.

Title: ______________________________

Prompt: Pick a piece of dialogue from your favourite film. Use this as the starting sentence for your exercise. Include cement.

Title: ______________________

Prompt: Write a story about an old key finally being used for its original purpose after a very long time. Include ink.

Title: ______________________________

Prompt: Write a story about a character who is extremely possessive of an inanimate object. Include deception.

Title: ______________________

Prompt: Write about a character who has gone blind and now has found their true passion in life as a result. Include chamomile.

Title: ______________________________

Prompt: Write about a therapy session that goes wrong. Include purple.

Title: ______________________

Prompt: Your character is in a bad mood for no reason, despite being a lovely person. Everything happening around them is going well.

Title: ______________________________

Prompt: Describe a day in the life of a character exactly ten years older than you. Include wood.

Title: ____

Prompt: Describe a day in the life of a character exactly ten years younger than you. Include a plant.

Title: ____________________

Prompt: Write a story about a character who has a passionate charitable cause and has found a way to make a real difference for that charity.

Title: ______________________

Prompt: Describe two characters who have an unusual way of settling arguments. Include a graduation ceremony.

Title: ____________________

Prompt: Write about a character fighting to overcome their worst fear.

Title: ______________________________

Prompt: Paint a picture of how someone would use the internet in twenty years' time.

Title:

Prompt: Write a snapshot interaction between an eccentric but proud parent and their child. Include something spherical.

Title: ______

Prompt: Pick an article in today's newspaper. Write a scene based on the setting and events in the article.

Title: ______________________________

Prompt: Two polite characters encounter a third character with a very foul mouth and uncouth manners. Include something fluffy.

Title: ______________________________

Prompt: Your protagonist is a musician encountering a mid-life crisis. Include an item not meant to be musical, but used to make sound.

Title: ______________________________

Prompt: Write a story that involves hearing voices in the mirror. Include a pillowcase.

Title: ______________________________

Prompt: Two strangers bond over their hair (this can include any hair, like beards). They have nothing else in common.

Title: ______________________________

Prompt: Write a story that takes place on a rubber dinghy. Include a tin of sweetcorn.

Title: ______________________________

Prompt: Begin your story with: "A herd of [something] approached on the horizon and we knew it spelled doom."

Title: ____________________

Prompt: Write a story that involves a small theatre putting on a film or play. Include red items.

Title: ____________________

Prompt: Your protagonist has a balance problem and a witty sense of humour. Include snow.

Title: ______________________________

Prompt: Deep in a remote cave, there's an 80s boombox about to be discovered. Include at least 5 characters.

Title: ____________________

Prompt: Tell a story from a different perspective, literally. Only describe what can be seen from a bird's eye view. Include a willow tree.

Title: ______________________________

Prompt: Describe the day in a life of someone who has always lived life on their own terms.

Title: ______________________________

Prompt: Write a story about the consequences of actions of your character from 5 years ago being felt today.

Title: ______________________________

Prompt: One character needs to extract a secret from another character for a noble cause. Include gold.

Title: ______________________________

Prompt: Write a story that involves jumping from a moving car. Include a dog.

Title: ____________________

Prompt: Your protagonist has been stranded in a forest. Include butterflies.

Title: ______________________________

Prompt: Describe the origin story of a radical hippy living in a geodesic dome.

Title: ______________________________

Prompt: Write a snapshot story about a family that loves each other but fails to communicate on any level.

Title: ______________________________

Prompt: Your protagonist sails a boat to a desert island. Include a 90s trend.

Title: ______________________________

Prompt: Write a story that takes place entirely in a hospital. Include socks.

Title: ______________________________

Prompt: Scientists have just figured out how to bottle talent, but the cost is high. Your protagonist can afford one bottle.

Title: ____________________

Prompt: Write a story in the style of an Alice in wonderland adventure, that takes place in a manor.

Title: ______________________________

Prompt: A mechanic finds her skills coming into use outside of work. Include coal.

Title: ____

Prompt: Write a story about an unusual friendship. Include a bathmat.

Title: ____________________

Prompt: Something does not smell good and the source of the smell reveals a mystery.

Title: ____

Prompt: Your protagonist has modest goals and is finally about to achieve their dreams. Finish the story before they can achieve them.

Made in the USA
Las Vegas, NV
01 December 2023

81888326R00061